# CONTENTS

*These «two types» drawn by Jon and published in 1943 are typical of the stereotyped British officer, phlegmatic and composed at all times, whatever the circumstances. This popular publication met with huge success during the conflict, thanks to its remarkably faithful caricature of the «so British» spirit.*

When the Allied troops landed on the Normandy coast on the 6th of June 1944, they were challenged by German divisions, the majority of which were undermanned and whose combat strength contrasted from one division to another, and was far from 1939 standards.

The successive setbacks since 1943, with the Afrika Korps debacle and the loss of Paulus' 6th Army in Stalingrad, had weakened the German Army.

Although, Great Britain had found itself alone in its combat against Germany and Italy, following the French capitulation, the situation was quite different in 1944.

The invasion of the USSR in 1941, together with the Japanese attack on Pearl Harbor in December 1941, enabled the British Army to count on two new and critical Allies for the outstanding conflict.

Due to the immensity of its territory, Russia was to prove an endless abyss for the Wehrmacht, which incessantly fed this front with reinforcements in order to compensate for its countless losses.

Meanwhile, the United States were to become the «arsenal of democracy» thanks to their industrial strength, which was entirely devoted to supplying the army. Indeed, as early as 1942, the production of civilian vehicles among others was ceased in favour of specific military vehicles.

From then on, the Americans began to provide their Allies with food, weapons, vehicles, planes and other miscellaneous supplies.

Russia was to greatly benefit from this support, in particular to re-equip and re-organise its efforts to successfully challenge Germany. In 1943, Stalingrad was the theatre of the decisive battle that was to mark the end of the German hegemony on Russian territory and the beginning of a long retreat, which 2 years later brought the Russians to Berlin. However, equipment could not compensate for the terrible human losses sustained by the Russians, and Stalin repeatedly called for a second front to be opened to reduce the German pressure.

And his wishes were put into action in December 1942, with the American landing in North Africa and the destruction of the Afrika Korps.

1943 was also to mark the Allied landing in Italy, however they progressed with difficulty for the Germans put up fierce resistance, despite the Italian capitulation.

*The original caption in German reveals that this group of grenadiers belonging to the 91st Armoured Division, and led by General Falley, fell under American paratrooper fire on the night of the 5th to the 6th of June during an ambush.*

An attempted landing in Dieppe in 1942 had resulted in the virtual annihilation of the British and Canadian troops on the beaches.

In the meantime, the Allies had taken the time to analyse the reasons behind this defeat, and had recovered substantial information on the German forces in France from the Resistance, finally agreeing, late 1943, to land, not in the Nord Pas de Calais region as initially planned, but on the shores of Lower Normandy, during the following year, 1944.

The Anglo-American armies now had the required logistics and infrastructure to succeed their operation, the most important in History. The operation's codename was OVERLORD and the aim was to successfully land 5 infantry divisions on the 6th of June, then 12 further divisions, among them armoured divisions, over the first week, with an ambitious objective of establishing a bridgehead the first day.

Furthermore, 3 airborne divisions were to be dropped with orders either to capture or to destroy bridges and to generate overall confusion aimed at hindering the progression of German units towards the beaches. The same mission was entrusted to the Allied Air Forces, which were to prevent the movement of troops by implementing massive bombing campaigns on road junctions (of which many Norman towns were to be the foremost victims) and by gunning German convoys.

*Hunting for souvenirs was a favourite pastime among the GI's and this one is no different. He has unearthed treasures from an officer's helmet to an armband, via a P 08 and a Browning GP 35.*

in fact transformed into a battlefield, where the Germans were to excel in the art of camouflage. By perfectly melting into the surrounding landscape, the grenadiers inflicted great losses on the Allies and halted the progression of infantry and armoured divisions, which laboriously made their way forward in this maze of verdure.

Field Marshal Rommel had failed to stop the Allies on the beaches and he had perfectly grasped how dangerous the Air Force could be, following the African debacle. It proved to be one of the determining factors of the conflict in the hedgerows thanks to observation craft which, overlooking the landscape, could control artillery fire, together with the intervention of fighter bombers, which prevented the progression of troops or vehicles by day.

This total command of the air space resulted in only 9 aircraft adorned with black crosses able to actually attack the allied bridgehead on the 6th of June. The others had been bombed down or damaged before reaching the zone.

On the evening of the 6th of June, the landing had been successful, however the Allies now needed to rapidly overcome the German divisions before they could counterattack. The Normandy bocage was to prove a terrible hindrance to the Allies and an advantage for the Germans, who had made the most of this peculiar terrain, hence compensating for their inferior numbers and equipment. Indeed, this typical landscape, shaped over the centuries by small fields separated by a number of hedgerows and woods, was

Nevertheless, the Battle of Normandy was to last up to the 22nd of August and only massive bombing campaigns such as Operation Cobra or Goodwood actually enabled the long-awaited breakthrough and the annihilation of the German resistance.

This book will offer you an insight into the equipment and materials used by the soldiers who fought on Norman soil. Many of them sacrificed their youth and their lives for what they believed to be the best of causes.

*In an orchard somewhere in Normandy, this British tank crew poses in front of its Sherman, the front of which is equipped with a blade to clear obstacles on the beaches. These «tank dozers» were specifically designed for the 6th of June. The turret on this one has been covered with camouflage netting and one of its crew members is holding a Sten gun.*

... " AVANT QUE NE TOMBENT LES FEUILLES ... "
CHURCHILL AVAIT PROMIS LA " LIBÉRATION "

W. CHURCHILL

..ET LES FEUILLES SONT TOMBÉES !

*Just one of the many handouts distributed by the authorities in Vichy, with an ironic caption referring to Winston Churchill's announcement of an imminent liberation.*

## From peace to war

The Japanese attack on the American fleet in Pearl Harbor on the 7th of December 1941 was a total and utter surprise.

Indeed, since 1939, following orders from France, the nation's industry had begun to produce the vehicles and planes that were painfully lacking in the French Army. Most of them were in fact delivered to Great Britain, following the 1940 defeat.

The American Military Staff was stupefied to witness the methods required and the speed at which France had been defeated in barely 2 months of fighting.

It has to be said that the neutral position adopted by the United States after World War I, was to result in a dramatic reduction in military orders during the 1930's. Thus, the American Army found itself, in 1940, underequipped with material that was both obsolete and unsuitable for the modern warfare of which the Germans had become the forerunners as early as the Polish campaign, with the simultaneous use of aircraft and armoured vehicles (Blitzkrieg).

However, let's not forget the Americans' great pragmatism. As early as 1942, industrial civilian production was brought to a halt to make way for military programmes and the manufacture of new and specific materials.

The United States very rapidly became the Allies' main supplier in the war against Germany.

The Liberty ship convoys brought both men and equipment to Britain, along with many supplies sent to the USSR via the Murmansk strait. The day before the landings, no less than 1,500,000 GI's were stationed on British soil.

And the soldiers who landed on the 6th of June were far from resembling their 1941 predecessors, who had barely changed since their forefathers of the Great War.

The M1917A1 helmet (similar to the British helmet with its typical «dishpan» shape) had been auspiciously replaced, late 1941, by the M1 helmet and the GI's silhouette had been totally transformed with a new uniform comprising an M41 blouson and mustard wool trousers. Their canvas equipment remained almost identical, however, in particular, the M1903 rifle was replaced by a semi-automatic Garand rifle, with its eight-round «en bloc» clip, offering excellent firing power in combat.

*Typical American soldier's uniform in 1941, identical to that of his forefathers during World War I.*

Just like the British Army, the American infantry was entirely motorised. Its vehicles were of recent design, however armoured vehicles failed to equal their German counterparts and it was in fact their great numbers on the battlefield that made all the difference.

But the Military Staff was also concerned about their soldiers' day-to-day life. Attacks were preceded by intense artillery fire with permanent aircraft intervention to prevent the progression of enemy troops, either by bombing positions or by gunning roads and hollow paths. For the wounded, impressive logistics were set up and the most seriously hit were operated on site, then transported to hospitals in Britain. Behind the lines, every effort was made to ensure their best comfort. Supplying the troops was a priority and it was efficiently carried out. One of the greatest surprises for the liberated civilians was to witness this vast profusion of resources and materials that the soldiers, very often, failed to even take the time to recover when leaving their stations.

*In the vicinity of St-Lô in July 1944, a group of GI's posing next to a destroyed Panzer IV.*

# American Ranger on the morning of the 6<sup>th</sup> of June

On the morning of the 6<sup>th</sup> of June, the 224 Rangers led by Lieutenant Colonel Rudder scaled the cliffs at Pointe du Hoc in order to destroy the 155mm guns in the nearby battery. The Rangers arduously advanced through the debris left by aerial bombing, to discover but empty emplacements, the guns having been hidden further inland. Over 2 days, the Germans counterattacked, decimating the Rangers who were forced to withdraw, such that by the 8<sup>th</sup> of June, only 120 men remained, the others having been killed or wounded.

Our soldier is a Sergeant from the 2<sup>nd</sup> Ranger Battalion and he is holding a bangalore, a tube filled with explosives designed to blow up barbed wire networks, among others. His uniform comprises an M41 blouson and a military vest. His trousers are made of sackcloth (originally a fatigue uniform) and, just like many other soldiers from elite units, he has managed to find a pair of paratrooper's boots. The armband on his left sleeve is a gas detector, which changes colour when in contact with the latter. And of course, he is wearing a lifebelt, for his kit is so heavy that he has no chance of swimming should he hit the water. Similarly, his gasmask, in its watertight cover, is always close at hand.

*MKII A 1 grenade with pressure-type firing device, which works similarly to a mine. A pressure of only 9kg is sufficient to activate the explosion.*

*MK II A 1 with pull-type firing device.*

*MK II A 1 with release-type firing device maintained by a weight of 1kg. The explosion is detonated when the weight is removed.*

*Defensive MK II A1 fragmentation hand grenade. Originally painted yellow, they became green as from 1942.*

*Military vest seen from behind with an M-1943 folding shovel. Note the M-1926 lifebelt and the British Toggle rope carried by certain units, in particular the 4<sup>th</sup> Infantry Division.*

## Paratroopers from the 82ⁿᵈ and 101ˢᵗ Airborne.

The Luftwaffe was the first to have successfully engaged parachute units as early as 1940, particularly during the capture of Fort Eben-Emael in Belgium.

Operations in Norway were also to prove the strategic relevance of this new weapon, which was far from leaving the American strategists indifferent.

The 501ˢᵗ Regiment was the first unit to be created in the United States in 1941.

The first operational jump was made during Operation Torch in Algeria in 1942. Then followed the 1943 landings in Italy, in which the recently founded 82ⁿᵈ Airborne Division took part.

The same year was also to mark the creation of the 101ˢᵗ (the Screaming Eagles).

These two divisions were dropped over Normandy on the night of the 5ᵗʰ to the 6ᵗʰ of June.

The principal aim of the 101ˢᵗ Airborne Division drop (mission ALBANY), comprising 6,800 paratroopers, was to control the 4

roads offering an exit from Utah beach and to destroy the artillery battery at St-Martin-de-Varreville.

The 82ⁿᵈ Airborne Division's mission (BOSTON) was aimed at taking Ste-Mère-l'Église and capturing the bridges to the east of the village (Chef du Pont and La Fière).

However, drops in the dark of night were generally rather scattered. Furthermore, the Flak was on the look-out, readily breaking up the waves of Dakotas.

Certain teams of pathfinders were unable to correctly mark out the jump zones; consequently a number of paratroopers found themselves totally isolated or at least far from their initial target. For the less fortunate, flooded areas proved to be deadly, for they were so heavily equipped that drowning was inevitable.

During the night of the 5ᵗʰ to the 6ᵗʰ of June, total confusion reigned, however, certain groups managed to reform, under the auspices of dynamic officers who recreated combat units capable of undertaking assigned missions.

Over 13,000 paratroopers were dropped that night.

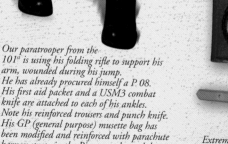

Our paratrooper from the 101ˢᵗ is using his folding rifle to support his arm, wounded during his jump.
He has already procured himself a P. 08.
His first aid packet and a USM3 combat knife are attached to each of his ankles.
Note his reinforced trousers and punch knife.
His GP (general purpose) musette bag has been modified and reinforced with parachute harness straps in the Rigger made workshops.

Fabric shoulder insignia of the 82ⁿᵈ Airborne Division.

Fabric shoulder insignia of the 101ˢᵗ Airborne Division, bearing the particularity of a white tongue.

Extremely practical engineers' wrist compass issued to parachute units.

Although the German units present in the sector were of no great combat value, the confusion generated by these massive parachute drops resulted in disorganised counterattack, for the paratroopers were scattered over a vast zone. The Americans suffered great losses due to this German resistance, but also due to the poor jumping conditions in the midst of the night. Troops who were transported by gliders also suffered major losses. For the Americans, the operation was a semi defeat, but from which they learned many a lesson for their future operations.

The airborne troops' combat uniform was slightly different from that worn by the land army in 1941. Indeed, for specific missions, the paratroopers needed clothing with a number of pockets and of more flexible use.

The uniform adopted in 1942 proved to be too fragile, hence the addition of leg and elbow reinforcements in certain companies, in particular those of the 82$^{nd}$ Division. In the same vein, regiment workshops (rigger made) created specific features for military clothing and equipment, such as additional ammunition pockets.

Certain troops, finding their uniform too light in colour for night operations, went as far as camouflaging it with paint. Paratrooper boots were also quite distinctive, in comparison to the ankle boots used by other armies.

*Escape kit containing a silk map, a compass and a saw, carried by pilots and issued to certain paratroopers.*

*Leather cavalry gloves for both pilots and paratroopers.*

*Cricket unearthed in 2004 on the site of a Dakota crash near Ste Marie du Mont.*

*Paratrooper from the 82$^{nd}$ Airborne Division, armed with a Garand rifle. His First Aid Packet is attached to his chest rig. He is wearing reinforced trousers and, in particular, Rigger made pouches produced in the UK and containing extra ammunition.*

## US helmets: From the M1917 to the M1

The 1917 Doughboy arrived in France with his boy scout-style helmet which, of course, offered no genuine protection against shrapnel.

The American Army very quickly adopted the British model which remained in service up to 1941, and was referred to as the M1917-A1 helmet.

However, even this new helmet did not efficiently protect the lower parts of the head.

Consequently, in 1941, a highly innovative helmet was developed, comprising a heavy steel one-size shell, with a lighter plastic helmet (liner) placed inside. Several improvements were made throughout the war, however the overall shape remained the same.

The chin strap on paratrooper helmets was modified in 1942, becoming an integral part of the liner, hence ensuring improved helmet support during jumping. They were referred to as USM2 helmets and were easily recognisable thanks to their crescent-shaped «D» chinstrap bales. However, their fasteners proved to be fragile, and they were replaced late 1944 by the M1C. The liner was also distinctive and recognisable thanks to an internal snap fastener for the entire chinstrap and two fabric triangles for the chin cup.

Apart from a few rare exceptions, soldiers tended not to camouflage their helmets, and if they did, it was generally limited to a net in order to disguise their uniform shape. On the contrary, in keeping with the corps spirit, the GI's readily decorated their helmets or liners with their division insignia or their own personal touch.

The following pages offer a few examples.

*The first compressed cardboard liners were too fragile and were replaced by plastic liners.*

*Heavy helmet used on the first hours of D-Day by the engineer units, who cleared the beaches of obstacles in order to facilitate the progression of the following waves of assault.*

*Light helmet (liner) bearing the insignia of the 2ⁿᵈ Infantry Division.*

*M1 steel helmet with the insignia of the 5ᵗʰ Infantry Division.*

*29th Infantry Division liner.*

*M2 nurse's helmet with the neutral red cross symbol.*

*M2 with the insignia of the 377th Field Artillery Battalion, attached to the 101st Airborne Division.*

*Nurse's helmet with the neutral red cross.*

*In the torment that reigned throughout Normandy, not even the red cross was spared, as seen on this helmet.*

*Helmet with its original camouflage net.*

*The US Captain's rank is painted on the front of this M1.*

*The French Captain's rank is soldered onto this 2nd Armoured Division M1 helmet.*

*Anti-shock helmet, specifically designed for tank crews and issued as from 1941, presented here with M-1938 goggles.*

## INDIVIDUAL WEAPONS

## The Garand rifle

In 1941, the majority of soldiers were still equipped with Springfield M1903 manual mechanism repeating rifles, with a bolt action system similar to that of the Mauser K 98.

In the late 1920s, tests were carried out on a semi-automatic rifle, leading to the production of the Garand M1, adopted in 1936. The United States were in fact the first nation to add such a weapon to its military arsenal. It was a gas-operated rifle with an 8-round en bloc clip-fed magazine, offering infantrymen an appreciable firing power against the enemy, the latter generally equipped with standard bolt-action rifles.

The conflict was to lead to the increased production of the Garand M1, with the subsequent relegation of the Springfield which, with the addition of a sight, was used by snipers. The Garand consequently became the infantry's principal firearm, however it required close maintenance and regular cleaning. Over 4 million rifles were produced throughout the conflict.

I have personally listened to many German veterans having fought against the US paratroopers with, often painful, memories of the advantage offered to the Americans by this rifle, when they themselves were armed with K 98 5-round stripper clip rifles requiring manual breech-loading…

*The Garand M1, the infantry's standard firearm.*

### The Garand M1

**Calibre:** 30-06 (7.62mm)
**Weight:** 4.37kg
**Feed system:** 8-round clip

*M1 bag containing the 4-part rifle cleaning rod and a rifle brush used for all 30 calibre weapons.*

*M7 grenade launcher used for streamer grenades.*

*M1 bayonet with its M7 plastic scabbard.*

*Comparison between these 2 rifles. The Springfield M-1903 was no longer used on the front, but it continued to arm those behind the lines. It was the standard 1917 Doughboy's firearm, later to be relegated to second place by the Garand in 1936. Both used 30-06 ammunition, however the Springfield was equipped with a 5-round stripper clip similar to the German Mauser.*

*Complete combat chest rig for a soldier armed with a rifle. The M-1923 cartridge belt could hold 10 clips and 8 bullets. The M-1910 shovel with its T-shaped shaft placed under the M-1928 haversack meat can pouch. The M-1942 canteen was attached on the left side, whereas the right side was reserved for the bayonet and the M-1942 First Aid Pouch.*

# USM1

Again in 1941, a carbine was adopted for soldiers who were not in direct contact with the enemy, such as drivers, telephonists, etc… It was the USM1 carbine, designed by Winchester, a semi-automatic, 7.62 calibre, gas-operated gun similar to the Garand.

A specific model, the USM1A1 with folding stock, was designed for the paratroopers, and exclusively produced by Inland. This carbine is extremely in demand today.

Six million USM1's were produced during the conflict by ten different manufacturers, including Winchester and Inland for the most commonly used, but also Underwood (a typewriter manufacturer) and Rock-Ola (renowned for its Juke Boxes!!!).

It should be noted that this weapon, which was extensively used by France in Indochina and Algeria, was only withdrawn from service in the 1980s, certain models still being seen in active service in documentaries on various conflicts throughout Asia and South America, hence offering firm proof of its excellent design.

| USM1 | |
|---|---|
| **Calibre:** Cal.30 M1 | |
| **Weight:** 2.5kg | |
| **Feed system:** 15-round magazine | |

*Wood stock USM1 with its canvas pouch containing 2 magazines.*

*USM3 fighting knife with its leather USM6 scabbard, issued to soldiers equipped with a USM1.*

*Folding stock USM1A1, specifically designed for paratroopers.*

# Colt 45

Just like its German counterpart, the Luger P 08, the legend of the Colt 45 was born during the 2 World Wars. Designed by the engineer John Moss Browning, the gun was adopted by the army in 1911 and small quantities were delivered as early as 1912. By the end of World War I, over 500,000 had been delivered.

The Colt 45 used during World War II was slightly different from its predecessor. The most remarkable difference was the replacement of its wooden grip by a plastic grip. Its name also changed: it became the Pistol Automatic Caliber .45 M1911 A 1.

It was a powerful firearm, capable of propelling a 15gr bullet at 900km/h. Enough to stop a charging bull! Its main drawback was its weight, however its many qualities, such as its power and reliability, were much appreciated by its users, to such an extent that the US Army only replaced it in 1982. A total of over 2.5 million Colt 45's were produced from 1912 to 1945.

*This Colt 45's original grips have been replaced with transparent plastic grips, enabling pictures of pin-ups to be slotted inside.*

*Ammunition was packaged in boxes containing 50 bullets.*

*M-1923 pouch housing 2 magazines.*

*Leather holster, which could be attached to a belt thanks to 2 hooks*

| Colt 45 | |
|---|---|
| **Calibre:** 45 (11.43mm) | |
| **Weight:** 1.1kg | |
| **Feed system:** 7-round magazine | |

## INDIVIDUAL WEAPONS

## THOMPSON submachine gun

Emblematic weapon used during the prohibition period and gangland killings, popularised by Hollywood, the Thompson submachine gun was created in 1921.

Its final aspect was established in 1928. Easily recognisable with its revolver handle and its 50-round drum magazine. Due to its high cost, a simplified version, the M1, was produced in 1943: among other changes, the charging handle was moved to the side and the revolver handle disappeared. It could now only use a 20 or 30-round magazine. This simplification offered an economy of 40% in production costs.

A fine quality weapon, it nevertheless had a limited range of 50 metres and was further penalised by its heavy weight, rendering carbines and Grease guns more popular.

However, its firing power, associated with its calibre rendered this gun a genuine danger for its adversaries in close range combat.

*Magazine pouch.*

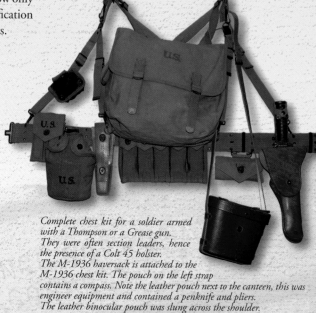

### THOMPSON

**Ammunition:** 45 ACP (11.43)
**M28:** 50-round drum magazine or 20/30-round box magazine
**M1:** 20/30-round box magazines
**Weight:** 5 kgs
**Rate of fire:** 700 rounds/min

*Complete chest kit for a soldier armed with a Thompson or a Grease gun. They were often section leaders, hence the presence of a Colt 45 holster. The M-1936 haversack is attached to the M-1936 chest kit. The pouch on the left strap contains a compass. Note the leather pouch next to the canteen, this was engineer equipment and contained a penknife and pliers. The leather binocular pouch was slung across the shoulder.*

*Thompson M-1A1.*

*Thompson M-1928 A1.*

# Grease gun M3 submachine gun

In 1943, in order to reduce the time and cost of production of the Thompson, the Ordnance Corps launched a new weapon, the M3, nicknamed Grease gun. Manufactured using stamping and soldering techniques (similar to the British Sten gun), it was far simpler to produce. Furthermore, its retractable stock offered a gain in terms of weight and bulk.

In its early days of service, it was unpopular due to its weaker firing power and its somewhat rustled up aspect, consequently being used as an onboard weapon in armoured vehicles. Distributed among a few units on the evening of the 5th of June, it rapidly met with the front lines, and finally proved to be much appreciated among its users.

A few changes were made in 1944, leading to the M3A1. A total of 650,000 guns were manufactured throughout the conflict.

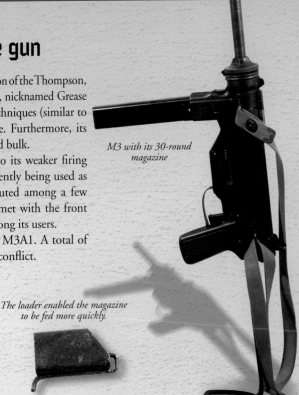

*M3 with its 30-round magazine*

## GREASE SUBMACHINE GUN

**Ammunition:** 45 ACP
**Feed system:** 30-round magazine
**Weight:** 3.7kg
**Rate of fire:** 400 rounds/min

*The loader enabled the magazine to be fed more quickly.*

# Bazooka M1 and M1A1

Adopted in 1942, the bazooka was in fact a simple tube open at both ends and equipped with handles, capable of projecting a 59mm hollow charge mortar thanks to an electric firing device. Initially used in North Africa, it proved to be effective against light armoured vehicles. Two models were simultaneously used, the M1 with 2 hand grips and the M1A1, adopted in 1943 with only one grip.

However, in Normandy, it could only destroy heavy armoured vehicles

## Bazooka M1 and M1A1

**Ammunition:** M6A1 59mm rocket
**Rate of fire:** 2 rounds/min
**Range:** 200m
**Weight:** 5.8kg
**Projectile speed:** 82m/sec

at close range, or, at best, immobilise them by targeting their tracking. The bazooka required a team of 2, a gunner assisted by a loader, hence offering more flexible use than an antitank gun, which was naturally more difficult to transport in a combat zone. Firing was only possible in open spaces, for rocket projection produced a long flame to the rear of the weapon. It should be noted that its successor, the M9, was not used in Normandy, but only in the Provence landings in August 1944.

## COLLECTIVE WEAPONS

# FM B.A.R. (Browning Automatic Rifle) M-1918 A2

Designed in 1916 and issued as from 1918, the FM BAR was a collective weapon capable of burst firing at a normal rate (550 rounds/minute) or reduced rate (350 rounds/minute).

It was a gas-operated firearm with locked breech, fed by a 20-cartridge magazine, with a maximum range of 1,200 metres. Nevertheless, its optimum firing power was at less than 60m. The principal change was made in 1937, with the addition of a bipod, the new gun being named the M-1918 A2 in 1940.

Similarly, its backsight adjuster came from the Cal. 30. A total of 168,000 guns were continuously produced up to 1945.

Its main shortcoming was that its magazine only contained 20 cartridges, however it proved to be a powerful and reliable firearm, offering excellent firing power to any combat group.

---

### FM BAR M1918 A2

**Ammunition:** 30-06 (7.62mm)
**Feed system:** 20-round box magazine
**Weight:** 8.82kg
**Rate of fire:** 350 to 550 rounds/minute

---

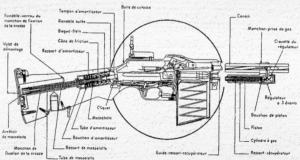

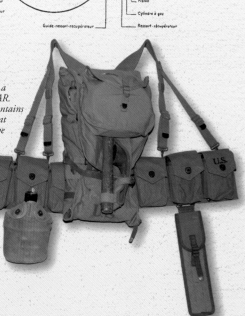

*Complete combat chest rig for a soldier armed with an FM BAR. The M-1937 cartridge belt contains twelve magazines. The tool that can be seen hanging outside the M-1928 haversack is an M-1910 pick-mattock. The satchel on the right-hand side contains a 4-part cleaning rod for Cal. 30 firearms. Certain soldiers armed with a BAR recovered nurses' chest rigs, which were larger than the standard rig, because of the extra weight of the magazines.*

# Browning M-1919 A 4 machine gun

In the 1930s, this gun superseded the M-1917 water-cooled machine gun. The fact that it was air-cooled offered this gun greater flexibility and it was used as much by the infantry as on vehicles. The A4 model was manufactured from 1942 with a total production of 425,000 guns. It was fed by 250-cartridge canvas belts, transported in metal cases, offering a rate of fire of 500 rounds/minute. It had a practical range of 1,000m. Its total weight, with the M2 mount was 18kg.

Used by the infantry with an M2 tripod, it could also be found on the majority of vehicles, on a variety of different mounts. Its ammunition was identical to that of the Garand or the Bar.

*Before the war, in the United States, a soldier proudly posing behind his M-1917 water-cooled machine gun.*

## Browning M1919 A 4 Cal.30

**Calibre:** 30-06 (7.62mm)
**Feed system:** 250-cartridge canvas belts
**Weight:** 14kg without the 18kg mount
**Rate of fire:** 500 rounds/min

*A 30 calibre mounted on a Willys Jeep with an M-1917 mount.*

# Browning M2 HB 50 calibre machine gun

Adopted in 1921, the 50 Calibre gun was to undergo a number of improvements in 1932, to become the M2. The letters HB stand for Heavy Barrel, due to barrel reinforcement for the air-cooling system. Just like the 30 calibre, flexibility was a major asset since the gun was used as much by the infantry as on vehicles (tanks, GMC…) or on planes (the P-47 was equipped with eight 50 calibre guns).

Using 12.7mm ammunition with a rate of fire of 500 rounds/min and an effective range of 1.8km, it proved to be an extremely efficient weapon against light armoured vehicles and troop concentrations. Its weight, however, was a potential drawback (72kg when loaded), but it could only be used with a fixed mount such as the M3 tripod or the M63 anti-aircraft mount, or on vehicles. It was fed with metal 105-round belts, transported in metal cases. The M16 version mounted on Half-Tracks and comprising four Cal. 50 turret guns for anti-aircraft defence is particularly worthy of note.

## Browning M2 HB Cal.50

**Calibre:** .50 BMG (12.7mm)
**Feed system:** metal 105-round belts
**Weight:** 55kg with the M3 mount
**Rate of fire:** 500 rounds/min

*Cal. 50 with its M3 tripod mount.*

## INDIVIDUAL EQUIPMENT

# Infantryman in combat gear

The combat uniform comprised an M41 blouson, a shirt and standard 1937 mustard wool trousers.

The M41 superseded the 4-pocket jackets introduced in 1926, which continued to be worn throughout the conflict as dress uniform, accompanied with a tie. The M41 blouson was lightweight and was a radical move from the combat uniforms of other belligerents thanks to its flexible use and its highly practical nature. Nevertheless, the M43 uniform was barely worn in Normandy and the Americans reverted to a 4-pocket jacket by late 1944.

Mustard trousers were issued both for combat and for dress uniform, as was the mustard shirt.

*GI posing for a souvenir picture in Great Britain before the landings. He is wearing an M-1941 blouson and cap adopted in 1941 as part of the service uniform.*

*A number of daily rations, from breakfast to dinner, together with a packet of cigarettes.*

*The US Army was rich and its soldiers were particularly well-equipped with supplies of all sorts. From top to bottom, match-boxes, tubes of toothpaste and other personal hygiene products and, finally, identity plates, one of which was always left on any fallen soldier; they were essential for identifying the dead.*

*A GI (his rank is Technician 5th Grade) from the 90th Infantry division armed with a Garand rifle, taking a breather during the fierce combat in Périers in Manche. The clip is clearly visible and readily at hand on his chest rig. Round his neck, he is carrying a bandoleer, containing other clips. His GP (General Purpose) musette bag to the side contains extra ammunition, but could also contain his personal belongings.*

*Individual M-1942 stove with its aluminium transport case. All efforts were made to ensure the best comfort for troops out in the field.*

## The last European rampart

In times of peace, the Army comprised the «Regular Army» comprising volunteers who enlisted for a period of 7 years. Then came the «Territorial Army» comprising volunteers who enlisted for 4 years during which they were given military instruction over and above their civilian job.

And finally, the «Supplementary Reserve» including soldiers having completed their service but remaining available for recall. Great Britain entered the war, along with France, on the 3rd of September 1939, following the German invasion of Poland. Voluntary enlistment was replaced by mandatory conscription for all men aged from 18 to 41 years. The BEF (British Expeditionary Force) that landed in France was a modern and entirely mechanised army, unlike France and Germany.

The hasty re-embarkation in Dunkirk in 1940, along with the armistice signed by France, were to leave many prisoners on the Continent, along with the entire arsenal of vehicles, their repatriation back to Britain having proved impossible. Up to 1941, the British were alone in their battle against the Axis powers. The Battle of Britain was to mark the very first genuine challenge against Germany's hegemony, but at a cost of major losses. The Lend-Lease programme, voted by the Americans, was nevertheless to offer the British Army new supplies, in the form of weapons and miscellaneous military equipment. Although pressure was somewhat reduced when the USSR entered the war in June 1941, it was only in December 1941 that the United States joined the conflict, which then became a World War. The British Isles were transformed into a formidable military barracks with an incessant flow of incoming American conscripts, preparing for D-Day. Since late 1943, the British Army was under the orders of the American General Eisenhower, whereas the British General Montgomery was in command of the invasion force reuniting, within the 21st Army Group, the 1st US Army and the 2nd British Army.

Consequently, on the 6th of June, 2 British infantry divisions (50th and 3rd) and one Canadian division (3rd) landed in Normandy. And in concrete terms, by midday, both the beaches and their inland access routes were under allied control. However, their key objective, the capture of the town of Caen, had not yet been achieved. The front was gradually stabilised to the north of the town and combat was fierce, particularly in Carpiquet, where the SS put up staunch resistance against the Canadian troops. Just like the Americans, the British-Canadian troops also

*The very first civilians posing with their liberators; the young boy has even recovered a military cap; unfortunately the insignia is impossible to identify. The soldier on the left-hand side is wearing a German belt.*

had to faced the Normandy bocage, where the Germans had become genuine masters in the art of camouflage. Intensive bombing was required to break their resistance.

The Allies, however, enjoyed both total command of the air space and an impressive superiority in terms of numbers. Furthermore, the British troops had been seasoned by 4 years of combat. Caen, which was but a mass of ruins, was finally totally liberated on the 19th of July, however it was only after operations Goodwood and Totalize that the German resistance was finally broken to the south of the town. Two months of intensive fighting had devastated the landscape. Each and every village had been bitterly defended and, often, only a few Panzer tanks actually made the difference on the battlefield. Attacks were preceded by intense artillery fire that was so powerful that certain German troops were later to describe it as the worst they had ever known, even when compared to the Soviet front.

The British and Canadian Armies had preserved their own uniforms, equipment and weapons with the exception of their vehicles which bore constant witness to the American support. Hence, their intensive use of Jeeps, Shermans…

The 22nd of August was to officially mark the end of the Battle of Normandy in Chambois with the closure of the Falaise Pocket and the junction between the American and Polish troops. However, victory was at a great cost, since 16,000 British and Canadian soldiers had lost their lives during these 2 months of combat.

*«British soldiers July 1944», this photo's original caption unfortunately offers little information on this group of soldiers. The soldier on the right is wearing a Leather Jerkin and an MK III helmet. To his right, his colleague is wearing 37 pattern battle dress and a General Service cap.*

## Infantryman in combat

Collection of standard issue cutlery, cans and knives.

Since 1937, the infantryman's combat gear, the 37 Pattern Battle Dress, comprised a woollen blouson with 2 chest pockets, closed by means of a chrome steel buckle at the bottom. Trousers had a large pocket in front and a dressing pocket on the right-hand side. The uniform was simplified (to reduce cost and manufacturing time) in 1940, becoming the (19)40 Pattern Battle Dress. Buttons were now visible and the pockets no longer had gussets.

Toiletries and shaving equipment.

Various sleeve insignia from British divisions having fought in Normandy. From left to right: 59th, 50th, 53rd and 15th Infantry Divisions. Below, a Green Howards shoulder patch.

This biscuit box has never been opened since January 1944.

Gas was a permanent threat and gas masks were always taken to the front lines. This model, equipped with a filter cartridge on the side, was in service as from 1943.

A number of standard issue metal boxes containing confectionery or cigarettes.

Tobacco was much appreciated during rest periods.

Soldier from the 3rd British Infantry Division, having taken part in the liberation of Caen in July 1944. Our soldier is wearing 37 Pattern Battle Dress and his regulation chest rig. Its pouches are filled with, among other ammunition, a light 2-inch mortar shell. He is wearing an MK III helmet, and is armed with an Enfield N°4 rifle, with a N°36 grenade on his belt. His canvas bandoleers contain extra clips for his rifle.

# Paratroopers: the 6<sup>th</sup> Airborne Division

Following the success of the German parachute units in 1940, the British Army decided to create identical units the same year. However, it was only in 1942 that they actually became operational during Operation Torch: the North African landings.

The 6<sup>th</sup> Airborne Division was created on the 23<sup>rd</sup> of April 1943, and was manned with 12,000 men by 1944. On the 6<sup>th</sup> of June 1944, the unit was entrusted with the mission of capturing the bridges over the River Orne (including Pegasus Bridge), along with the Merville artillery battery in Calvados. The division was placed under the orders of Major General Gale.

Major Howard's men attacked Pegasus Bridge at 0:21 hours, after being transported by 3 gliders which landed nearby, and the Café Gondrée became the first French house to be liberated. Ranville was liberated the same night. The attack on the Merville battery was entrusted to the 9<sup>th</sup> Battalion, led by Lieutenant-Colonel Otway, which partially succeeded in neutralising it following fierce combat throughout the night. Reinforcements continued to flood in, transported by gliders, and by 6:00 hours, around 4,000 paratroopers had set foot on Norman soil. It was also during the same night that the Orne bridges to the east of Troarn were destroyed.

The front was stabilised by the 12<sup>th</sup> of June and the paratroopers continued fighting up to the 16<sup>th</sup> of August across a defensive line conditioned, in part, by the Bavent woods to the east of Caen. The Battle of Normandy was to cost the division 4,457 men, 1,748 of whom were killed.

*Fairbairn sykes dagger issued to commandos and paratroopers: a formidable weapon when in the hands of an elite soldier.*

*Bavent woods to the east of Caen. A paratrooper from the 6<sup>th</sup> Airborne Division taking a moment's respite during combat against the 21<sup>st</sup> Panzer Division. His helmet has been camouflaged with hessian. Beside him, a leg bag attached to the ankle during jumps and containing a Sten MK V and a shovel for preparing the first positions.*

## Canada at war

Canada declared war on Germany on the 10th of September 1939. Mandatory military service was introduced in 1940 for all male citizens aged from 19 to 45 years.

Canadian combat gear was identical to the British Army, with the exception of the olive drab and improved quality. Both equipment and weapons were identical, hence enabling supplies to be rationalised since they were interchangeable.

The Canadians' first war effort proved to be dramatic since it involved the attempted landing in Dieppe in August 1942. Of the 5,000 men who landed, only 2,200 returned to Great Britain.

The beach zone assigned to the Canadians on the 6th of June 1944 was codenamed JUNO BEACH, and was located amidst the British landing zone. The 3rd Infantry Division, under the orders of Major General Keller, landed between Graye-sur-Mer and St-Aubin-sur-Mer. Combat was intense, however the small town of Courseulles was liberated and the Canadians continued their advance inland. Unfortunately, the Carpiquet airfield, their initial D-Day objective, could not be reached the same day. As early as the 7th of June, units were challenged by the 12th SS Panzerdivision Hitlerjugend, which had been brought to the battlefield the previous day.

*The last letter from Private Glen Francis Yost from the Queens Own Cameron Highlanders, killed in combat during the capture of St-André-sur-Orne. His name is among those engraved on the Bayeux Memorial, opposite the cemetery, in memory of lost soldiers. Curiously, a letter sent to his family by the officer in charge of his unit explains that he had been buried in a cemetery, along with his fellow soldiers who had fallen to the south of Caen. Undoubtedly due to a post-war error, Glen's body was never formally identified.*

The area to the north of Caen was to become the theatre of a battle which proved to be as unyielding as it was merciless, for certain Canadian prisoners were assassinated by the SS, particularly in Ardennes Abbey.
The 1st Parachute Battalion was dropped with the 6th Airborne Division and fought, in particular, in the Bavent woods.

*The Yost family in 1942, at the occasion of Glen's enlistment.*

*His small pack, unearthed in an antique fair in 2005, enabled me to trace his family who kindly offered a photograph of this soldier who had taken such care to identify his bag. Born in 1922, enlisted in 1942, he was killed on the 22nd of July 1944, after having arrived in Normandy 14 days earlier, on the 8th of July.*

# Combat uniform

Tam O'Shanter bearing the insignia of the North Nova Scotia.

Tam O'Shanter bearing the insignia of the Highland Light Infantry of Canada.

Sleeve insignia belonging to the same soldier.
The blue rectangle is the insignia of the 3rd Canadian Infantry Division.

By the evening of the 6th of June, 14,000 Canadians had landed and losses totalled 1,074, of whom 359 had been killed.

The town of Caen was liberated on the 19th of July, at the cost of its destruction, however the fighting was far from over. Indeed, the plain between Caen and Falaise was to be the theatre of a furious battle which was finally concluded with the closure of the Falaise Pocket on the 22nd of August. Many Canadian soldiers fell in places which were later to become famous such as the Verrière crest, or in the villages of May and St-André-sur-Orne, which had been fortified by the Germans.

Throughout the Battle of Normandy, the 2nd and 3rd Canadian Infantry Divisions lost a total of 18,444 men, 5,300 of whom were killed.

*Infantryman from the 2nd Infantry Division's Régiment de la Chaudière. His uniform is identical to that of his British counterparts, but is of better quality. He is carrying a WS 38 radio for short range liaison. Beside him, a kit bag belonging to Trooper Ken Johnson who took part in the Normandy campaign within a reconnaissance unit.*

Various sleeve insignia (Title) for Canadian units stationed in Normandy.

Ken Johnson's route, carefully written on his bag.

21

## From the MK II to the MK III

The MK II was the British regulation helmet throughout the conflict, more commonly known in France under its nickname of «dishpan». It was identical in shape to the MK I, used during World War I, and was adopted as from 1938. The liner was fixed by means of a nut and screw attachment at the top of the dome and there was an anti-magnetic trim along the border. The original chinstrap, made of fabric and equipped with springs, was replaced in 1943 by a flexible chinstrap, also of fabric but easier to produce.

This helmet was replaced in 1943 by the «tortoise-shaped» MK III, massively distributed among the assault troops on the 6th of June, particularly the Canadian units. This improved MK III helmet offered better protection, particularly on the sides of the head,

however the MK II continued to be concurrently issued up to the end of the war.

It is interesting to note that, the esprit de corps being ever-present, soldiers regularly painted or applied transfers to their helmets, bearing the colours of their regiment or unit.

They were generally not paint-camouflaged but by means of netting or hessian which masked their distinguishable shape.

Paratroopers were issued with a specific helmet in 1942, equipped with a leather chinstrap and a shock absorber at the base of the dome. The outer shell of this helmet was identical to those used by motorcyclists and tank crews – only the interior was different.

*Gunner's MK II helmet.*

*MK II helmet belonging to a Beach group unit, recognisable thanks to the white stripe.*

*MK II from the REME (Royal Electrical and Mechanical Engineers).*

*MK II helmet bearing the insignia of the 11th Armoured Division's Fifth and Forfar Yeomanry.*

*MK II bearing the insignia of the 2nd Canadian Infantry Division's Calgary Highlanders.*

*MK II belonging to the 3rd Canadian Infantry Division's Canadian Scottish Regiment.*

*MK III belonging to the 3rd Canadian Infantry Division's Regina Rifles.*

*MK III bearing the insignia of the 3rd Canadian Infantry Division's North Nova Scotia Highlanders.*

*MK III helmet from the 3rd Canadian Infantry Division's Cameron Highlanders of Ottawa.*

*MK III from an engineers unit.*

*MK III belonging to a Canadian artillery officer.*

*RAC helmet bearing the insignia of the 1st Polish Armoured Division.*

*RAC (Royal Armoured Corps) helmet.*

*Found in Normandy, this MK I paratrooper's helmet has successfully kept its secret, for its unit is impossible to identify.*

*Early model of the paratrooper's helmet with a fibre band along the edge The insignia belongs to the 6th Airborne Division's 7th Battalion Parachute Regiment (Somerset Light Infantry).*

*Paratrooper's helmet bearing the insignia of the 6th Airborne Division's 6th Airlanding Brigade (brought to Normandy by gliders).*

## The 1$^{st}$ Polish Armoured Division

Created in Scotland in 1942, the 1$^{st}$ Polish Armoured Division comprised men who had escaped combat in Poland in 1939 and in France in 1940, together with Polish volunteers from across the globe. Their uniform and equipment was British, however they kept their own insignia (Polish eagle) and their distinctive ranks, in particular the black left epaulette (in memory of the 1939 conflict).

The Division landed in Arromanches and Courseulles on the 2$^{nd}$ of August 1944, under the orders of General Maczek. The unit was to prove particularly efficient during fighting to the south of Caen and the closure of the Falaise Pocket. From the 19$^{th}$ to the 21$^{st}$ of August, it tenaciously held Hill 262 (Montormel), from where its tanks bombarded the retreating German troops. (F. Cybulski).

*Tank crew member from the Royal Armoured Corps. The Title is easily recognisable, as is the insignia on his typical armoured crew black beret.*

*Guard Division fabric sleeve insignia.*

*Royal Armoured Corps cap badge.*

*Mark II binoculars.*

*Member of a 1$^{st}$ Polish Armoured Division tank crew listening to one of his fellow soldiers. He is wearing the lightweight Tank Denim Suit, much appreciated by tank crews, for the summer temperatures in August 1944 were difficult to bear inside armoured vehicles.*
*His Enfield revolver holster and canvas ammunition pouch are visible in the foreground. The original sand colour was whitened giving way to this greenish hue.*

*RAC holster for an Enfield 38, specifically designed for armoured vehicle crews.*

*British tank crew member also wearing the canvas uniform. A dressing is attached to his right shoulder in case of emergency. British Armoured Divisions suffered greatly before the German units who were often equipped with more efficient military material.*

## Individual anti-tank weapons and grenades

When the British declared war, their standard anti-tank weapon was the BOYS rifle, adopted in 1937 and totally obsolete by 1939. This firearm, inspired by the American 12.7mm gun, proved to be totally ineffective against German armoured vehicles and was replaced in 1942 by the PIAT (Projector Infantry Anti Tank) with a calibre of 89mm.

Decidedly more difficult to handle than the bazooka, the PIAT was nevertheless an efficient weapon, having proved its worth particularly during a failed German attempt to capture Bretteville l'Orgueilleuse where Panther tanks from the 12th SS were ruthlessly beaten and destroyed by PIAT fire. However, handling its ammunition required strict attention.

*PIAT seen from the right.*

*This somewhat poorly preserved PIAT was unearthed in 2007. Torn to shreds by a shell, it remains a poignant reminder of the fighting that tool place over the summer of 1944.*

### Characteristics

**Calibre:** 89mm hollow charge
**Weight:** 14.5kg
**Effective range:** 100m
**Rate of fire:** 2 rounds/min

*PIAT seen from the left.*

*The anti-tank glass «stunt grenade» was smashed against the side of armoured vehicles, to explode 5 seconds later. Beside it, a rare example of its transport case.*

*The PIAT's hollow charge ammunition.*

*A N°80 phosphorous grenade.*

*N°82 «gammon» grenade.*

*A N°73 phosphorous grenade.*

*A N°36 segmented body grenade.*

*Offensive N°69 grenade with plastic body.*

## INDIVIDUAL REGULATION WEAPONS

### Handguns

*Enfield N°2 MK I* revolver.*

### Characteristics

**Calibre:** 0.380 (9mm)
**Weight:** 765g
6-cartridge cylinder

The Enfield N°2 MKI* was the standard issue revolver, and was distributed as from 1938, to be replaced in 1942 by the simplified MK I**. It was a reliable firearm, essentially issued to tank crew with a specially designed holster, and to officers and soldiers who were not obliged to carry a rifle.

Along with this gun, the British also used the Colt 45, in particular for its commandos, together with the 9mm Browning GP 35, produced in Canada.

### Rifles

In the early days of the conflict, British soldiers were still armed with Enfield N°1 MK III SMLE rifles, an inheritance from the Great War. It was replaced in 1942 by the Enfield N°4 MK I, of which 5 million pieces were produced up to 1945, including 24,000 specially designed sniper guns. It was manufactured in Great Britain, Canada and the United States.

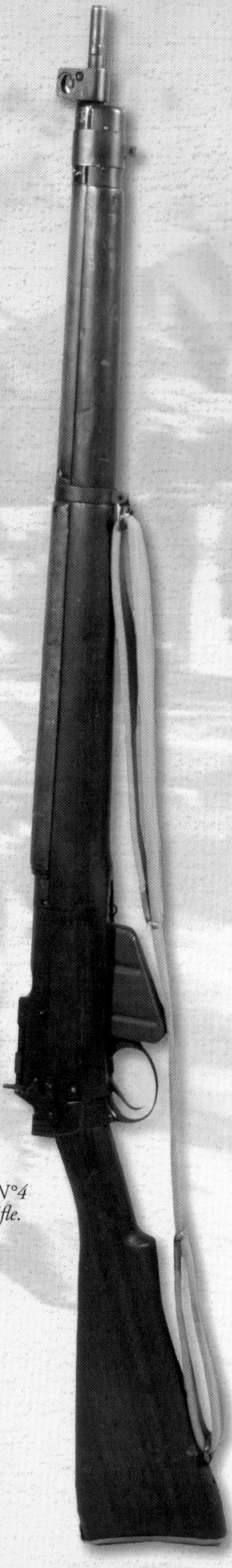

### Characteristics

**Calibre:** 0.303 inches (7.7mm)
**Length:** 113cm
**Weight:** 4.1kg
**Feed system:** 5-round stripper clip

*Enfield N°4 MK I rifle.*

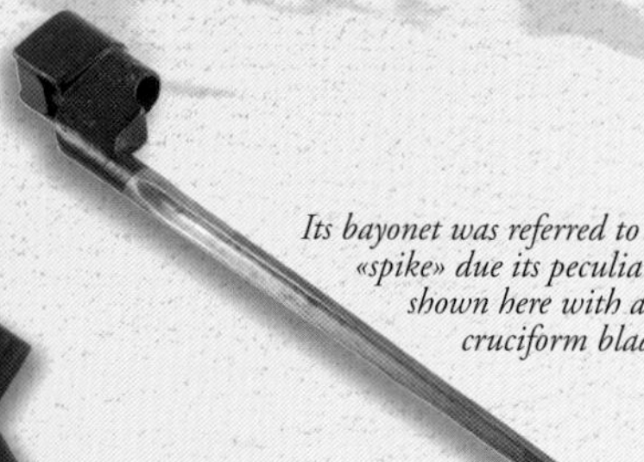

*Its bayonet was referred to as a «spike» due its peculiar shape, shown here with a rare cruciform blade.*

# Submachine guns

At the start of the war, the British Army had no automatic firearms; consequently, it hastily ordered Thompson M28 submachine guns from the United States. The first British submachine gun was only developed in 1941: the Sten MK I, a total of 100,000 of which were produced by 1942, when it was replaced by the MK II, of simpler manufacturing design. It must be said that this was a rather rudimentary weapon, produced by a stamping and soldering technique, and only actually comprising two machined parts, hence its low cost of around £1. Three adaptable stocks were available, however only 2 (tubular and skeleton) were used in Normandy. 1943 was to mark the arrival of the MK III, easily recognisable thanks to its receiver and barrel shroud machined in one single part. The rifle could no longer be dismantled, hence avoiding accidents due to poor tightening. Finally, paratroopers had the privilege of being issued with a far better finished Sten, the MK V, with a stock and revolver handle, together with a wooden front grip. The barrel was fitted with the Enfield N°4 rifle sight and a mount for the spike bayonet was even added. It is interesting to note that many MK II and MK III guns were passed on to the Resistance. A total of 3,750,000 Stens were produced up to 1945.

*Wooden case for transporting 9mm ammunition.*

*Sten MK III with a tubular stock, camouflaged for use out in the field.*

*Sten MK II with its typical skeleton stock covered with parachute rope.*

*Sten MK III with tubular stock painted green for camouflage.*

*Paratrooper's Sten MK V. The Enfield N°4 sight is visible, as is the bayonet mount.*

## COLLECTIVE WEAPONS

## BREN MK I machine gun

In May 1935, the British Army adopted, and built under licence, the Czechoslovakian FM ZGB-34 which was renamed BREN and replaced the LEWIS machine gun. It was put into service in 1937. The BREN was a reliable gas-operated weapon, and was used throughout the entire conflict. Its barrel was interchangeable and cartridges were placed in a box magazine above the breech block. The MK II appeared in 1941 and can be distinguished by a number of manufacturing simplifications. It was used by a 3-man team: a squad leader, an artilleryman and a gunner. The BREN could be used with a tripod, particularly in anti-aircraft defence, but also when mounted on BREN-CARRIER tracked vehicles. A total of 280,000 guns were produced up to 1945.

*The FM BREN could be used on a tripod, however its 30-round magazine feed system proved to be a handicap compared to the German MG's, fed by 250-cartridge belts and offering longer burst firing time.*

*Maintenance kit, shown both closed and open with the many tools required to ensure the gun's efficient operation.*

*This bag was transported by the artilleryman and contains parts and a replacement barrel.*

### Characteristics

**Calibre:** .303 (7.7mm)
**Weight:** 10.2kg
**Rate of fire:** 500 rounds/min
**Feed system:**
30-round magazine

*This BREN has also been camouflaged with 2 different shades of paint. In the field, magazines were also painted green, rather than their original black colour. The web sleeve at the end of the barrel is the dust cover.*

# VICKERS MK I heavy machine gun

The Vickers originated from the MAXIM machine gun, adopted by the German (MG 08) and Russian (Mle 1910) Armies. A standard British Army weapon since 1921, it was used by gunner battalions on the front lines in Normandy. Penalised by its heavy weight, it was not an efficient offensive weapon, however it proved its defensive value thanks to its water cooling system offering long and sustained burst firing. It required a 3-man team: a gunner assisted by a loader and an artilleryman who transported ammunition cases.

The visible difference between the WWI model and the one used during WWII concerned the cooler which was originally fluted, later to become smooth, accompanied by a canvas protection sleeve.

*A Vickers as it was installed in the trenches…*

*The Vickers was fed by metal cases containing 250-round canvas belts.*

## Characteristics

**Calibre:** .303 (7.7mm)
**Weight:** 10.2kg
**Rate of fire:** 500 rounds/min
**Feed system:** 250-round canvas belts
**Cooling system:** water - using a 4-litre cooler.

*Can used to cool the gun's 4 litres of water. This one bears specific identification markings.*

*Wooden case including the Vickers' cleaning and maintenance equipment.*

## The French Resistance

Following the defeat of the French Army in 1940, the government, led by Marshal Pétain, engaged in collaboration with Nazi Germany. However many men and women refused such surrender and, as early as 1940, acts of sabotage were perpetrated against the occupying troops. General de Gaulle, following his appeal on the 18th of June, and refusing defeat, encouraged the French people to resist. The very first networks began to develop early 1941, however it was only in June 1941, with the invasion of Russia, that the French Communists massively joined forces in a resistance movement. Between 1940 and 1944, no less than 260 networks were developed. Initially, their action was limited to acts of sabotage, but, as from 1943, their aim moved towards collecting information in order to inform the Allies of the German forces and, in particular, of the defensive elements comprising the Atlantic Wall.

*FFI (Forces Françaises de l'Intérieur, or French Forces of the Interior) parading throughout a recently liberated town.*

*Resistance fighters could finally come out from the shadows.*

Indeed, the Resistance was to play a crucial role in preparations for the landing operation, its agents successfully dispatching to London a number of plans of the fortifications that lined the Normandy coast. However, repression was merciless and many resistance fighters were shot down or deported.

On the night of the 5th to the 6th of June, personal messages sent by the BBC informed resistance networks of the various acts of sabotage that were to hinder the arrival of enemy troops on the Norman front. However, their action was to generate many reprisals, the most dramatic of which was undoubtedly the massacre of the innocent inhabitants of the village of Oradour-sur-Glane. It is interesting to note that, following the liberation, many resistance fighters enlisted in the 2nd Armoured Division and continued their combat as far as Germany itself.

*Evocation of the Resistance. The weapons used by the Resistance were taken from stock that had been hidden in 1940, dropped by means of parachute, or stolen from the enemy, such as this MP 40 and these stick grenades. The buckle on the German belt has been carefully denazified by filing down the swastika. The armband bears the various insignia worn after the Liberation.*

## Soldiers in combat

*In April 1943, soldiers from the 352nd Infantry Division's 1st KP Div Füs Btl 352 pose during an exercise in Tilly-sur-Seulles.*

The German soldiers who were present in Normandy in June 1944 were far removed from those that had victoriously marched through Paris 4 years prior.

The best divisions had been sent to the Eastern Front, where most of them had been annihilated. Defence of the Normandy coastline relied essentially on the fortifications comprising the Atlantic Wall, troops playing an essentially static role. Furthermore, several divisions were manned by soldiers who were either relatively old or very young, barely out of military school. Experienced troops were painfully lacking and, in order to complete certain units, Russian «volunteers» (Osttruppen) had been brought in. Their combat value was highly contrasting but generally low.

There were, however, a few exceptions, such as the 352nd Infantry Division, stationed in the Omaha beach sector. Seasoned on the Russian front in 1943, the division comprised trained troops from the Panzer Lehr Division, equipped with modern material.

Similarly, the lack of experience among certain divisions was compensated for by their extremely fervent motivation. Such was the case of the 12th SS, formed of young Hitlerian recruits (Hitlerjugend) aged 17 to 18. This division was placed under the command of officers with 4 years of wartime experience, particularly on the Eastern Front, and the Canadians in particular were to realise, at great expense, their immense potential during the bloody battle to secure the town of Caen.

But, primarily, the Allies were to face soldiers from different armies, which were divided as follows on the Western Front in June 1944:

865,000 men in the Heer (land army)

326,000 men in the Luftwaffe (German air force comprising, in particular, Felddivisions and paratroops)

102,000 men in the Kriegsmarine (navy, including many troops stationed in blockhouses)

102,000 men in the Waffen SS

To which were added the 25,000 Osttruppen.

As for material, there was a great diversity in terms of both weaponry and vehicles. Despite the stereotype image of a strong and fully motorised German Army, exclusively equipped with Tiger tanks, let us not forget that many units used horse-drawn transport and that the counterattack on the 6th of June was made possible thanks to French armoured vehicles, captured in 1940.

The Allies had total command of the surrounding air space and resupplying, both in fuel and ammunition, was a daily dilemma for the German troops.

Hence the importance of camouflage, be it for vehicles or men, and the Germans proved to be masters in this art, readily and literally melting into the Normandy bocage. For the Wehrmacht, combat was essentially defensive and the capture of Caen, as the American breakthrough in Saint-Lô, was only made possible thanks to dense bombing capable of breaking all resistance. The rare German counterattacks, such as Mortain for example, met with failure due the great Allied artillery strength and the omnipresence of their air forces, halting any vehicle movement by day.

The Battle of Normandy officially came to an end on the 22nd of August 1944 in Chambois, where the German 7th Army, encircled in the Falaise Pocket, lost the great majority of its military equipment. It is estimated that some 640,000 German soldiers took part in the 2 months of fighting, losses amounting to approximately 200,000 killed and 250,000 prisoners.

However, most of the German troops had managed to escape from the Falaise Pocket, and the same men fought during the Ardennes Offensive (popularly known as the Battle of the Bulge), and up to the German capitulation on the 8th of May 1945.

*Paratrooper with his helmet and specially designed camouflage blouson.*

## The Heer Infantry LANDSER in field uniform

*The infantry moving towards the front. In Normandy, only rare columns were able to progress as such, for the Allied air surveillance prevented any movement by day, which was consequently only possible under low clouds.*

The Wehrmacht was the German regular army and comprised three main constituents: the Heer, the Luftwaffe and the Kriegsmarine. They were all answerable to the High Command: The OKW (Oberkommando der Wehrmacht), placed under the orders of Field Marshal Keitel from 1938 to 1945.

To the West, the Heer reunited 2 Armies, comprising a total of 32 Infantry Divisions: General Dollmann's 7th Army, with its 161,000 men, ensured coastal defence from the River Loire to the Dives, whereas General Von Salmuth's 242,000 man-strong 15th Army, stationed from the Dives to the Escaut, comprised 18 divisions. Finally, the Army Group B, whose headquarters were in La Roche Guyon, was in fact a combination of the two aforementioned Armies, and placed under the command of General Field Marshal Rommel. The latter was then under the direct orders of General Field Marshal von Rundstedt, the supreme commander of the land forces on the Western Front. This illustrates the complexity of the chain of German command, for Von Rundstedt was only in fact in command of land forces and could effectively give orders to the commanders in chief of neither the Luftwaffe nor the Kriegsmarine. And this complexity was indeed to hinder German decision-making during the early hours of D-Day.

As for our Landser (term used to designate a German soldier), he very much resembled his forefather from the 1914-1918 trenches.

His uniform, adopted in 1936, comprised trousers and a jacket and was repeatedly simplified throughout the war. His helmet was a Stahlhelm 35, although the older Stahlhelm 16 continued to be issued to units behind the lines, but with a new interior.

His belt (Koppelschloss) was equipped with 3-compartment cartridge pouches (Patronentaschen) adopted in 1911 for the cavalry, together with a bayonet (Seitengewehr 84/98) for soldiers armed with a Kar 98 rifle. Then came the bread bag (Brotbeutel 31), to which a canteen (Feldflasche 31) or even a pan (Kochgeschirr 31) was attached, followed by a shovel (Spaten) in a specific pouch. All of the above was maintained in place by the heavy chest kit (Y-Reimen 39). The gas mask (Gasmaske 38) was carried on the back in a metal case. The tent sheet (Zeltbahn 31) could be attached to the rucksack (Tornister 39) when carried, but during combat, it was often attached to the top of the bread bag or hooked onto the assault kit (Sturmgepack) along with the pan.

As for boots (Marschstiefel), they had been replaced in 1943 by laced ankle boots (Schnurschuhe) and gaiters to economise on leather.

*Contrary to the entirely motorised Allied armies, several German units still used bicycles. This Landser is carrying his kit on his regulation bike. The metal case hanging under the crossbar can contain and MG case or even stick grenades housed in a special rack.*

Over and above the regulation field equipment, German soldiers also carried a multitude of personal items, distributed throughout the pockets of their jacket or in their rucksack. These civilian items enabled them, among other uses, to maintain links with their families. They essentially included toiletries, photographs or writing material for keeping in touch.

However, tobacco and leisure games were also part of their day-to-day lives. Evenings were spent playing Skat (a card game) or chess. Others preferred reading, or writing home.

These few objects, left by the German soldiers, offer us an insight into their daily occupations.

*Between exercises, free time was spent writing, or playing Skat and chess. As a matter of interest, these games were unearthed in 1996; they had been stored inside a gas mask case.*

*2 song books.*

*The Brotbeutel along with its contents.*

*Various packets of cigarettes.*

*Spectacle case.*

*Box of chocolates*

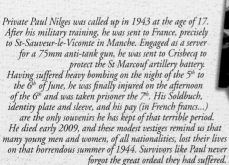

*Sewing kit*

Private Paul Nilges was called up in 1943 at the age of 17. After his military training, he was sent to France, precisely to St-Sauveur-le-Vicomte in Manche. Engaged as a server for a 75mm anti-tank gun, he was sent to Crisbecq to protect the St Marcouf artillery battery.
Having suffered heavy bombing on the night of the 5th to the 6th of June, he was finally injured on the afternoon of the 6th and was taken prisoner the 7th. His Soldbuch, identity plate and sleeve, and his pay (in French francs...) are the only souvenirs he has kept of that terrible period.
He died early 2009, and these modest vestiges remind us that many young men and women, of all nationalities, lost their lives on that horrendous summer of 1944. Survivors like Paul never forgot the great ordeal they had suffered.

## German helmet (Stahlhelm 35) and its camouflage

Inspired by the M1916, which had been massively distributed during the Verdun offensive, this new helmet, adopted in 1935, was an improvement on its predecessor.

Lighter and more compact, it offered a better field of view in lying position.

There were three different versions. Firstly, the M1935, produced during peacetime and extremely well finished. It was light green, its aeration eyelets were attached and it bore insignia on its side: a shield with the national colours on one side and an eagle holding a swastika in its claws on the other. After the Poland campaign, a directive ordered that the shield be removed to improve camouflage. Similarly, the original colour was too conspicuous and it was decided that helmets should be painted in a darker green, which was also a means of covering the insignia. Only in the Luftwaffe, a few rare helmets remained with both insignia and their light grey colour.

Following the early days of the conflict, the first simplifications were applied to the helmet in 1940 in order to enable mass production. They then became dark green and their eyelets were directly stamped and no longer attached. The eagle insignia continued to be applied to the sides.

Finally, in 1942, a third model was produced, with a border that was no longer rolled but stamped.

The paratroopers were issued with a specially designed helmet in 1938.

During the Battle of Normandy, all of the above were used along with the M1916. However, their characteristic feature was undoubtedly the many different camouflaging methods used to ensure that they go unnoticed in the Normandy bocage. The Waffen-SS tended to prefer helmet covers, and only a few rare examples of camouflaged helmets could be found in these units.

*M1916 helmet reconditioned with an M1931 interior.*

*Heer M1923 with an eagle on the left side.*

*The right side of the same helmet with a shield bearing the national colours (black, white and red).*

*M1935 adorned with a 1st model Luftwaffe eagle.*

*The same helmet but with a 2nd model eagle.*

*This Heer M1940 served on the Eastern Front; originally painted white, it was subsequently repainted dark green. The white colour can be seen on certain areas.*

Waffen-SS M1942 with
runes on the right side.

The left side was adorned with this
insignia up to the middle of the war.

Three-tone camouflaged M1940; the
insignia is still visible under the paint.

SS helmet with helmet cover.

Heer helmet with helmet cover and
original camouflage netting.

Another SS helmet with helmet cover.

Camouflaged Luftwaffe
M1942 helmet.

Camouflage was applied by hand by the
soldiers themselves; it is therefore rare to find
two identical helmets, although three shades of
paint were often used.

Paratrooper's helmet with 2-tone
camouflage, typical of Von der
Heydte's 6th Regiment.

The same helmet with a 2nd
model Luftwaffe eagle.

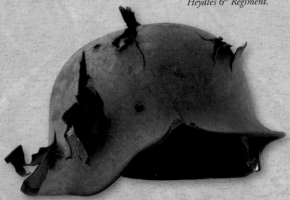

This M1940 was found in a house behind Hill 112, literally torn
to shreds by shellfire. One barely dares to imagine what became of
the soldier who was wearing it.

## Camouflage on equipment and material

Contrary to the Allies, the Germans, having lost control of the air space, used camouflage as an essential constituent of their defence and protection.

Thus, vehicles were swathed in foliage, often resembling genuine bushes on wheels. The grey paint used in the early days of the war was replaced by sand yellow as from 1943, hence enabling green and ochre camouflage paint to be applied on top.

In motorised units, painting was applied using pneumatic paint guns, however, in many cases, personal initiative and inspiration were behind hand-painted camouflage using brushes… and nothing escaped, from vehicles to pans, via individual firearms.
The aim was, of course, to literally melt into the Normandy bocage.

Here is an array of camouflaged equipment, illustrating the great diversity of the art.

*2 M1931 pans.*

*2 MG cases. Since camouflaging was an individual art, subject to no particular instructions, many variations could be found. The lower case was used to transport 100mm cartridges. This type of camouflage was typical of the Reichswehr (predecessor to the Wehrmacht) and can be found on many cases dating from 1936-1937. Camouflage was generally factory-applied and consequently of more uniform inspiration.*

*Gas mask cases were no exception.*

*Metal case for 50mm mortar shell.*

*Binoculars and case, with 2-tone paint camouflage.*

*Of course, vehicles were also disguised, like this metal motorcycle satchel and DKW NZ 350 motorcycle speedometer.*

# Sergeant (Unteroffizier) MG squad leader

The MG team comprised an artilleryman, in charge of ammunition cases and the pouch containing the machine gun's replacement barrel, a gunner and a non-commissioned officer acting as squad leader and responsible for commanding firing after having identified targets. We know that our Sergeant is a veteran, thanks to the ribbon of his Eastern Front Medal (Ostmedaille), passed through his buttonhole, along with his 2nd Class Iron Cross ribbon (Eisernes Kreuz II Klasse), a medal that was never worn on the uniform, contrary to the 1st Class, which he is wearing on his left pocket, since insignia were worn during combat.

The white border on his collar and shoulder boards informs us of his rank. A rank that offers him the privilege of being armed with an MP 40 (Maschinenpistole 40) of which the canvas magazine pouches are also in evidence. He is carrying a folding shovel (Klappspaten 38), adopted in 1938, along with a map pouch (Meldetasche 35). His Sturmgepack can also be seen on his back. His helmet and gas mask are both camouflaged with the characteristic 3 shades of paint used in the Normandy countryside (sand, ochre and green), hence enabling him to «disappear» amidst the bocage.  A stick grenade (Stiehlhandgranate 24) has been slipped under his belt and he is also carrying a combat knife, attached to his boot.

*Unteroffizier (Sergeant) from a 352nd Division infantry unit.*

*Regulation torch.*
*The leather straps were used to fix it to one of the jacket buttons.*

*The canvas Sturmgepack rucksack contained the regulation K98 cleaning kit, a sweater and a reserve iron ration.*

*Compass (Marschkompass).*

*The Sturmgepack, which literally translates as assault kit (shown here in an all-canvas model), was attached to the chest rig as seen on the top photograph.*

*M1933 field telephone (Feldfernsprecher 33).*

## COLLECTIVE WEAPONS

*In Siouville in Manche (Mont Odile in the background), a soldier from the 709th Infantry Division is posing with his MG 42, mounted on an anti-aircraft defence tripod.*

As from the very beginning of the conflict, the German Army used the MG 34 (Maschinengewehr 34) machine gun, which proved suitable for a number of different missions. Indeed, equipped with a heavy mount (Lafette 34 tripod) and a telescope sight, it was used as a heavy machine gun (SchweresMG), however its air cooling system did not allow long burst firing for its rapid rate of fire could deform its barrel. Another tripod (Dreibein) was used for anti-aircraft fire.

Finally, equipped with a bipod, it became a light machine gun (LeichtesMG) and was, as such, easily transportable during offensive operations. An extremely accurate firearm, it was, however, costly to produce and required attentive cleaning and maintenance. Hence, in 1942, it was superseded by the MG 42, manufactured by stamping and soldering, and consequently, simpler, faster and cheaper to produce. Its rate of fire was further improved, but, what appeared initially as a quality could also prove to be an inconvenience for this gun literally devoured ammunition. This excessive ammunition consumption meant that German soldiers were overburdened with cartridge belts and cases. However, the MG 42's firing power commanded a certain degree of respect among its adversaries, who easily recognised it thanks to its «zip fastener» noise. Yet, supplying soldiers on the front was a constant struggle, for the Allied fighter planes wereomnipresent,bombarding all enemy vehicles.

*An MG 34 on an anti-aircraft defence tripod (Dreibein 34). The following material is attached to hooks on the tripod legs: a drum magazine, a magazine belt (Gurtrommel 34) with 2 drums, and a sand yellow pouch containing the MG's maintenance equipment. At the foot of the tripod, a metal case with 2 oil and fuel cans for cleaning. Note the «P» on the cover, in order to avoid confusion with ammunition cases.*

*The gunner's bag contained all of the necessary equipment for the upkeep of his weapon.*

*MG 34*

## MG 42

**Calibre:** 7.92mm
**Weight:** 11.5kg
**Feed system:** identical to the MG 34
**Rate of fire:** 1,300 rounds/min

*MG 42*

Our gunner, a Private (Gefreiter), is equipped with a special kit containing all of the tools required to clean and maintain his MG. He is also armed with an automatic pistol, generally a P 08 or a P 38. Round his neck, he is wearing smoked anti-dust goggles, frequently seen on period photographs. His easily accessible individual torch is held in place on his shoulder board button. The rest of his equipment is similar to that of a regular soldier. He is wearing 4-pocket canvas battledress, originally a fatigue uniform but used here as a combat uniform due to the hot Normandy summer.

*An MG 34 used as a heavy machine gun (SchweresMG) mounted on a tripod, during the French campaign in 1940. The gun crew can be seen, including the artilleryman, the gunner and the squad leader.*

*MG 42 on its heavy tripod (Lafette 42). In German, the MG was given two different names depending on its use. When mounted on a bipod, it was referred to as a light machine gun (LMG or LeichtesMG), whereas, on a tripod, it became a heavy machine gun (SMG or SchweresMG).*

*Bag for transporting cases.*

*The MG's 7.92mm ammunition had more powerful gunpowder than the K98 Mauser, hence the reminder on the ammunition cases (für MG).*

*The case, with an E (Ersatzteilkasten) marked on the top contained wearing and replacement parts. They were packed inside this case in small metal boxes.*

## Officers from the HEER

These 2 officers, an Infantry Captain (Hauptmann), recognisable thanks to the white border on his cap and his shoulder boards, and an Artillery (red stripe) Sub-Lieutenant (Leutnant), are working on a regulation map table.

After the Poland campaign in 1939, orders were given for officers' uniforms to bear a closer resemblance to those worn by soldiers and to render them less conspicuous to enemy snipers.

Thus, our Hauptmann is wearing a 1943 field blouse (Feldbluse) bearing his rank insignia. On his belt, he is carrying a magazine pouch for the MP 40, and a

P 08 holster. His high boots were worn during combat, along with his jodhpur-style trousers.

On the table, we can see field telephones (Feldfernsprecher 33) and a TORN.E.b radio receiver. The Leutnant is wearing a non-regulation jacket made of camouflaged tent canvas. From his posting in Russia, he has kept a Soviet PPSH submachine gun. He is also carrying an LP 42 signal pistol with a pouch containing flares of different colours.

During combat, his cap was of course replaced by a steel helmet.

Signal pistols: to the left 2 Walthers, the top one appears to have suffered intensive use, judging by the colour of its barrel. To the right, a wartime model: the LP 42.

Canvas bag (leather was also used) containing flares for the signal pistol.

Officer's brown leather belt with a two-tongued buckle.

Pair of 6x30 binoculars (Dienstglas) with 2 bakelite cases.

Infantry officer's collar patches.

Shoulder boards, to the left an Infantry Leutnant, and to the right a Captain Doctor (Hauptmann).

Panzer Division Major's shoulder boards (pink border).

*During the combat around Caen, 2 officers take stock of the situation and prepare their next operation.*

# Heer tank crew

During World War I, the Germans had failed to fully exploit the potential offered by tanks. However, between the wars, General Guderian, among others, developed combat theories in which armoured vehicles were the key offensive constituent.

In 1939, the Blitzkrieg had demonstrated the relevance of these theories and armoured weapons consequently became the Wehrmacht's spearhead during its future campaigns in France and Russia.

The 21st Panzerdivision was the only armoured division present on the 6th of June 1944, most of its tanks being of French origin. The division was involved in many a counterattack against the British paratroopers. A further 4 Heer tank divisions arrived on the scene much later. They were the 2nd, the 9th and the 116th PzDiv, along with the PanzerLehr, the best equipped of the Heer divisions employed on the Norman front. Then came the 5 Waffen SS armoured divisions, particularly well equipped with modern material.

The Panzer IV was the basic tank used in armoured units, each division being endowed with several vehicles. However, the Panthers and, of course, the formidable Tigers were the most feared by the Allied tank crews, their 8.8cm guns leaving them virtually no chance of victory.

*Adjutant Bronikowski was killed in April 1945, an infantryman after the destruction of his Panther. Having escaped the Kessel von Falaise (Falaise Pocket), he was awarded the Iron Cross 1st Class, along with the Tank Combat Badge.*

*With his headphones in place and his electric laryngophone plug in his hand, this tank crew member is also carrying 10x30 binoculars.*

*With his typical black uniform and double-breasted jacket, this tank crew member has just left his tank and, looking rather worried, is about to embark on a reconnaissance mission.*

*Panzer officer's cap, recognisable thanks to its pink border.*

*Black tank crew cap (Feldmütze 43).*

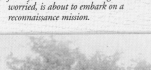

## INDIVIDUAL WEAPONS

During World War II, the Wehrmacht had to ensure the control of a vast territory stretching from Russia to France, whilst maintaining its presence on African soil. This massive deployment of both men and materials resulted in the systematic use of weapons and equipment seized from conquered or occupied territories. Alongside regulation weapons, a variety of rifles or handguns originating from a number of European military arsenals could be found. However, procuring sufficient supplies of ammunition of all origins and all calibres proved to be problematic. Front line troops were generally issued with regulation weapons, but those in non-fighting units, along with foreign soldiers donning the German uniform (the Osttruppen for example) were given weapons of a number of origins from Soviet to French, via Italian for example.

## Handguns: P 08 and P 38

The P 08 was adopted by the British Army in 1908 and was the most widely used handgun during world War I. Its career was to continue between the wars to end up, inevitably, in the hands of the Wehrmacht. An extremely accurate and finely finished gun, it was to suffer no negligence, requiring thorough maintenance, which was to lead the Germans to look for an equally accurate weapon, but of a more rudimentary design, in keeping with feasible conditions of use in times of war. They called upon Walther, the company behind the P 38, adopted on the 26th of April 1940. This double-action mechanism pistol was to gradually outrun the P 08 (of which production was ceased in 1942), with a total of 1,250,000 guns produced throughout the conflict.

### Characteristics of the P 08

**Calibre:** 9mm
**Weight:** 855g
**Feed system:**
8-round magazine

### Characteristics of the P 38

**Calibre:** 9mm
**Weight:** 900g
**Feed system:**
8-round magazine

## Submachine guns

The MP 38 was initially and prioritarily issued to paratroopers and armoured vehicle crews. As the conflict progressed, it was more widely distributed among a number of units thanks to its simplified production (having become the MP 40). Generally intended for the squad leader, it proved to be more efficient than certain Allied firearms, with the exception of the PPSH 41, of decidedly more rudimentary design and, above all, fed with a 71-round drum magazine. Around 1,000,000 MP 38 and MP 40 guns were produced.

### Characteristics of the MP 40

**Calibre:** 9mm
**Weight:** 4.7 kg with full magazine
**Feed system:** 32-round magazine
**Rate of fire:** 500 rounds/min
**Range:** 100-200 metres

## MP 44

A small quantity of MP 44 assault rifles could be found. A revolutionary weapon at the time, it combined both the accuracy of a rifle and the rate of fire of a submachine gun. Furthermore, it was machine stamped, hence enabling its mass production. After the war, the Russians produced a replica of this gun which they called AK 47.

### Characteristics of the MP 44

**Calibre:** 7.92mm
**Weight:** 4,6kg
**Feed system:** 30-round magazine
**Rate of fire:** 500 rounds/min

# Karabiner 98 K (kurz) rifle

The Karabiner 98 K (kurz) rifle Just like its predecessor, the G 98 used during WWI, the K 98 was the standard issue rifle for German troops from 1939 to 1945. It was referred to as a Karabiner, rather than a Gewehr, because of its shorter barrel (60cm compared to the G 98's 74cm). Adopted in 1935, its was present on all fronts until May 1945 and no alterations were made apart from the odd simplification to increase production. The Wehrmacht also used a number of captured K 98's, countries such as Belgium and Poland having produced them under licence during the pre-war years. Over 15 million rifles were produced.

## Characteristics of the K 98

Calibre: 7.92mm
Weight: 3.9kg (with the pre-war walnut stock) or 4.2kg (with the wartime glue-laminated stock)
Feed system: 5-round stripper clip
Rate of fire: from 10 to 15 rounds/min depending in the firer's dexterity
Range: 500m

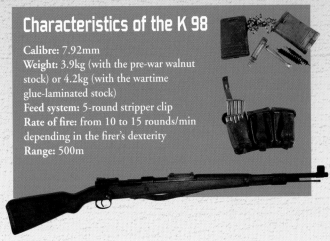

# G 41 semi-automatic rifle

During the first weeks of war against Russia, the Germans were surprised to discover the SVT 40 semi-automatic rifle, which totally outclassed the K 98. Indeed, this gas-operated rifle no longer required manual bolt activation, offering an undeniable advantage during combat. The companies Mauser and Walther very quickly set to designing an equivalent, the latter finally producing the lion's share (128,000 G 41 W's produced by Walther, compared to 1,673 G 41 M's produced by Mauser).

## Characteristics of the G 41

Calibre: 7.92mm
Weight: 4.7kg
Feed system: 2 stripper clips each containing 5 rounds
Rate of fire: 20 rounds/min
Range: 600m

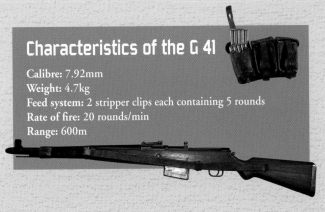

# G 43 semi-automatic rifle

To improve on the imperfections noted on the G 41, Walther designed the G 43, which was lighter, more reliable and less costly to produce.
The magazine was detachable and the gas system only concerned part of the barrel. Approximately 400,000 were produced, over 50,000 of them equipped with a ZF 4 telescopic sight.

## Characteristics

Calibre: 7.92mm
Weight: 4.3kg
Feed system: 10-round magazine
Rate of fire: 30 to 40 rounds/min
Range: 600m

## The LUFTWAFFE land troops

On the Western Front, the Luftwaffe was answerable to the OKL (Oberkommando der Luftwaffe), commanded by GFM Hugo Sperrle, whose headquarters were in Paris. Their missions included the surveillance and defence of the air space using radar and anti-aircraft defence units (the FLAK). Of its 300,000 men, the majority were posted in Flak batteries, for German aviation was virtually inexistent on the Western Front. Most squadrons were posted in the USSR or scattered across Germany to counter the massive Allied bombings. Hence the intervention of only 9 aircraft on the 6th of June. However, the Luftwaffe also comprised paratroopers, in particular the 6th Regiment, commanded by Von der Heydte, which fought against the American paratroopers in Carentan.

*Luftwaffe soldier wearing his blue uniform, in particular the characteristic jacket: the Fliegerbluse.*

Similarly, many Flak troops found themselves posted in land combat units, referred to as the Luftwaffe Felddivision. Their camouflage dress included a blouson which was simpler than those used by the paratroopers. The basic uniform and canvas equipment were blue, and the jacket (Fleigerbluse) had 2 pockets with concealed buttons.

Our soldier is armed with a Panzerschreck, copied from the American bazooka, a few of which had been recovered in North Africa. With its 8.8cm ammunition, it proved to be a formidable weapon against Allied tanks. The Felddivision was operational on land alongside other Heer and SS units. At the beginning of the war, leather equipment was brown (like the boots our soldier is wearing) with the LBA (Luftwaffe Bekleidungs Amt) stamp, which literally translates as Luftwaffe clothing office. Two divisions fought in Normandy: the 16th Division, which challenged the British to the south of Caen, and the 17th Division, posted in Seine Maritime, facing the Americans to the north of Eure-et-Loir.

*Luftwaffe Soldbuch, in which all information concerning the soldier was noted. It served as a paybook and personal identification. It was carried by soldiers, contrary to the Wehrpass, which was kept at the barracks.*

*Cap*

*Combat knife issued to all land troops.*

*Stick grenade (Stiehlhandgranate 24) and egg grenade (Eihandgranate 39), the 2 most widely used grenades in the German Army.*

*Late June 1944, the Luftwaffe was sent to Normandy, where it lost over 75% of its men during combat with British troops. Armed with a Panzerschreck, this soldier is enjoying a moment's respite between 2 attacks. He is wearing an M1943 cap, and has placed his helmet on the ground; although camouflaged, he has taken care to preserve the eagle insignia.*

# The LUFTWAFFE paratroopers

The paratroopers were elite units and had forged their reputation during combat in May and June 1940, thanks to audacious raids, but also, and in particular, during the capture of Crete in 1941. Their victory was however at a cost of many men and planes. And it was also the reason for the paratroopers being posted in land-based units for the rest of the war. To the west, the parachute divisions (2$^{nd}$, 3$^{rd}$ and 5$^{th}$) were reunited within General Meindl's II FJ Korps. Only Major Von der Heydte's Fallschirmjäger-Regiment 6 was in Normandy on the 6$^{th}$ of June 1944, and it counterattacked its Allied counterparts from the 101$^{st}$ Airborne Division in the Ste-Mère-Eglise – Carentan sector. The 2$^{nd}$ FJDivision maintained its posting in Brittany, whereas the 3$^{rd}$ and 5$^{th}$ FJD's engaged in combat, challenging the Americans in Manche, around St-Lô in particular.

The paratroopers' basic uniform was the standard Luftwaffe blue wool uniform. However, they were issued with a variety of specific equipment including, first and foremost, their helmet and camouflaged jacket. They were also issued a significantly higher number of automatic firearms than other Wehrmacht fighting units. However, what was to strike the American soldiers was their great fighting spirit, thanks to intensive training and a genuine esprit de corps, associated with the pride of belonging to an elite unit.

*This paratrooper is armed with a Kar 43 with its specific magazine pouch. The 2-tone camouflage on his helmet is typical of the 6$^{th}$ FJR that fought against the Americans, in Carentan in particular. He is wearing an uncamouflaged bandoleer housing his K 98 stripper clips, along with 2 bags around his neck to carry stick grenades.*

*The specifically designed camouflaged bandoleer contained stripper clips for the K 98.*

*The flick knife was issued to all personnel using a parachute. Indeed, its blade and bodkin were useful for cutting or disentangling the suspending ropes. On land, it also proved to be an excellent combat knife.*

*Canvas gas mask pouch.*

*This paratrooper has just been taken prisoner and he is still carrying his MP 40 round his neck. However, his adversaries will waste no time in disarming him.*

## The Waffen-SS

The Waffen-SS was a military branch of the SS (Schutzstaffel) comprising the SD and the Allgemeine SS.

Upon its creation in 1934, it was a paramilitary force designed to help the Nazi regime to assert its power through force and the elimination of any opposition. Its characteristic feature was its extremely severe selection criteria: by order of priority - racial (the candidate was to have no Jewish origins), political (he was to be a convinced Nazi) and finally physical, with specific rules with regard to height and weight among others.

These units were given excellent military training, together with ideological instruction that was to create a powerful esprit de corps.

The Waffen-SS was officially created on the 8th of March 1940 and, at the time, it only comprised 3 divisions that were to participate in campaigns in Poland, Belgium and France.

Even in these early days, prisoners and civilians were victims to acts of violence.

1942 was an important year, for the divisions were transformed into entirely motorised armoured divisions, endowed with the best available equipment. Hence, the SS-Schutze became the SS-Panzergrenadier.

The 6 main divisions were present in Normandy, most of them having earned themselves a reputation on the Eastern Front, and despite the previous 3 years of intensive combat

that had decimated the ranks, their fighting spirit remained intact.

Troops were placed under the orders of seasoned veterans, much to the disadvantage of occasionally inexperienced Allies. With armoured vehicles that were far more effective and resistant than those of their adversaries, they literally blocked the Allied advances, particularly before Caen. The fighting on Hill 112 (south of Caen), or in St-Lô, was of rare violence and losses were proportionate to hostilities. Hence, of the 20,000 men comprising the 12th SS in May 1944, only 8,000 successfully fled from the Falaise Pocket 4 months later, leaving behind all of their equipment.

Although similar to that of the Heer, their uniform in fact had many differences.

The eagle was sewn onto the left sleeve and collar runes replaced the Litzens. The belt buckle bore the inscription: «Meine Ehre heisst Treue» i.e. «My Honour is called Loyalty». But above all, the SS were to rapidly adopt camouflaged clothing, including the Tarnjacke, worn above the jacket, along with helmet covers. In May 1944 camouflaged combat uniforms appeared and were prioritarily issued to the 12th SS (Hitlerjugend).

Their weapons were identical to those used by the Wehrmacht. However, the Waffen-SS was to commit many acts of violence, due to the fanatical personality of its members. Thus, 115 Canadian prisoners were callously assassinated in Ardennes Abbey to the north of Caen. Not forgetting the 2nd SS Panzerdivision's («das Reich») slow advance to the front in June 1944, sullied with many hangings and, in particular, the massacre and destruction of the village of Oradour-sur-Glane.

*Sniper armed with a K 98 equipped with a ZF41 telescopic sight. The sight's transport case can be seen on the soldier's belt. His equipment was kept to a minimum and included magazines, binoculars and a combat knife. His camouflaged jacket (Tarnjacke) enabled him to melt into the surrounding vegetation.*

# SS-PANZERGRENADIER 12th SS PANZERDIVISION « HITLERJUGEND »

*Before the D-Day landings, members of the 1st SS PzDiv (LAH) enjoying a beer at the terrace of a café. The tank crew member in the centre is wearing a black uniform, different from his fellow soldiers who are wearing feldgrau combat uniforms. Portrait of another member of the LAH (Leibstandarte Adolf Hitler), recognisable thanks to the monogram on his shoulder boards.*

*Examples of SS insignia From top to bottom, black shoulder blade with the strap upon which the LAH monogram was applied, armbands with the division name, collar patches.*

This division, created in 1943, comprised young recruits from the Hitler Youth, of an average age of 18. They were under the orders of experienced troops from the 1st SS PzDiv «LAH», having fought for two years in the USSR.

The division arrived on the outskirts of Caen on the 7th of June and halted the Canadian advance on Carpiquet. Nicknamed the «baby division» by the Allies, they actually proved to form a formidable adversary, for these indoctrinated (many were born in 1926, whereas A. Hitler came to power in 1933) and fanatical soldiers preferred sacrificing their lives rather than surrendering.

By the 14th of August, only 500 of the division's infantrymen remained.

*This tank crew member is wearing a black leather jacket taken from the Italian Navy stock. The black fabric trousers are, however, his own.*

When it was founded, the division took advantage of the Italian defection, recovering large quantities of Italian camouflaged drape which, thanks to skilled tailors, was transformed into battledress, hence compensating for the lack of Tarnjacke, among others. It was one of the characteristic features of the division's uniform. Our gunner is wearing a long jacket made of the same fabric which was originally lined with rabbit skin for use on the Eastern Front. This one, found in Normandy, has had its fur removed for use as an overjacket. He is carrying the basic gunner's equipment and is serving an MG.

*Gunner grenadier wearing an overjacket made of Italian camouflaged fabric. He has camouflaged his helmet with fine netting in order to mask its conspicuous shape. His P 38 holster can be seen on his belt, along with its maintenance pouch. His pockets are filled with stick grenades.*

## Military insignia and decorations

Just like the Soviet soldier, the Landser wore his military decorations on his jacket during combat. The most familiar is, of course, the Iron Cross, of which there were several classes.

However, wearing combat insignia was, first and foremost, a matter of pride for these soldiers who were keen to illustrate their bravery to others. Here are a few examples:

*Infantry Officer decorated with: Iron Cross 2nd Class (ribbon on his buttonhole), Iron Cross 1st Class, Infantry Assault Badge and Black Wound Badge on his chest pocket.*

*Iron Cross 2nd Class (Eisernes Kreuz). During combat, only the ribbon was worn on the jacket buttonhole.*

*Iron Cross 1st Class in its box.*

*Arm campaign shields awarded to soldiers having fought in the associated region (Kuban to the left and Demjansk to the right).*

*Deutsches Kreuz (German Cross) introduced in 1941 to reward soldiers already donning the Iron Cross 1st and 2nd Class. It was worn on the right chest pocket.*

*Close Combat Clasp (Nahkampfspange) introduced in 1942, of which there were 3 classes: bronze (15 days hand-to-hand combat), silver (30 days) and gold (50 days).*

*Wound Badge (Verwundeten Abzeiche) introduced in 1939 and awarded to soldiers who had been wounded once or twice in combat. There were 3 classes: black (1 or 2 wounds), silver (3 or 4 wounds) and gold (5 wounds or more).*

*War Merit Cross (Kriegsverdienstkreuz), introduced in 1939 and awarded to non-fighting personnel.*

*Eastern Front Medal (Ostmedaille) awarded to soldiers having suffered the winter of 1941 in Russia.*

*General Assault Badge (Allgemeines Sturmabzeichen) introduced in 1940 and awarded to soldiers from units other than the infantry and having taken part in over 3 days of combat.*

*Infantry Assault Badge (Infanterie Sturmabzeichen) introduced in 1939. There were 2 classes: (bronze and silver) and it was awarded to soldiers having taken part in over 3 days of combat.*

*Panzer Assault Badge (Panzerkampfab-zeichen) introduced in 1939 and awarded to troops having taken part in 3 different days of armoured combat. There were 2 classes (bronze and silver).*

*Heer Flak Badge (Heeres-Flak-abzeichen) intro-duced in 1941 and awarded to soldiers from the Heer having taken part in at least 5 days of combat.*

*Luftwaffe Flak Badge – the eagle is different from that on the Heer Flak Badge.*

*Sports Badge.*

*Horseman's Badge.*

*Parachutist Badge (Fallschirmschütze-nabzeichen) awarded after 5 jumps.*

*The same badge, in fabric, was sown on the jacket.*

*Luftwaffe Ground Assault Badge (Erdkampfabzeichen) introduced in 1942 and awarded to Luftwaffe personnel having taken part in infantry combat.*